Practise and Pass

Cambridge
Young
Learners
English
Test

STARTERS

Pupil's Book

GW00728809

Cheryl Pelteret
and Viv Lambert

DELTA Publishing
Quince Cottage
Hoe Lane
Peaslake
Surrey GU5 9SW
United Kingdom
www.deltapublishing.co.uk

First published 2010

Project managed by Chris Hartley
Edited by Barbara MacKay
Designed by Peter Bushell
Illustrations by Claire Mumford and Andy Hammond
Printed by

ISBN: 978-1-905085-36-1

Contents

Step 1 – Prepare

1 Listen and number the pictures. 1

a

b

c

d

e

f

g

h 1

2 Ask and answer.

What's number 1?

It's a ruler.

3 Find and write the words from exercise 1.

1 ...... ruler ......

2 ......

3 ......

4 ......

5 ......

6 ......

7 ......

8 ......

c	v	k	l	p	x	s	p	d	g
o	r	u	l	e	r	m	e	l	v
m	j	h	q	b	c	i	n	e	k
p	v	b	o	a	r	d	c	a	w
u	o	d	r	x	c	t	i	i	g
t	p	l	o	w	i	d	l	d	p
e	g	b	m	p	w	l	s	i	d
r	u	b	b	e	r	m	g	l	e
y	s	n	u	n	l	b	h	t	s
j	h	g	i	u	c	b	o	o	k

4 Look and write the words.

1 There's a ___rubber___ .
2 There are two _____ .
3 There's _____ .
4 _____ .
5 _____ .

5 Look and write the words.

1 There's a **k o b o s a c e**. ___bookcase___
2 There's a **r e c e t a h**. _____
3 There's one **w o d i w n**. _____
4 There are three **h a c i r s**. _____
5 There's a **r o d o**. _____
6 There's a **p u b a d c o r**. _____

6 Write the words.

1 There are twelve ___pencils___ on the cupboard.
2 There's a _____ next to the window.
3 There are two _____ under the bookcase.
4 The _____ is in front of the board.
5 There's a _____ behind the door.
6 There are three _____ on the table.

Step 2 – Practise

1 Look at the picture on page 7. Put a tick ✔ or a cross ✗.

1 [✔] There are three books on the table.

2 [ ] There's a picture on the wall.

3 [ ] There are three chairs in the classroom.

4 [ ] There's a pencil on the chair.

5 [ ] There are books on the floor.

6 [ ] There's a computer in front of the window.

Draw ticks like this.

2 Listen and draw lines. 🎧 2

1   2   3   4   5   6

Draw lines like this.

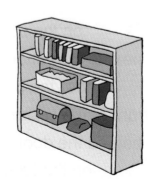

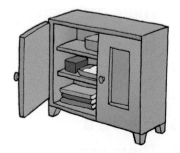

Step 3 – Pass!

1 **Listen and draw lines.** 🎧 3

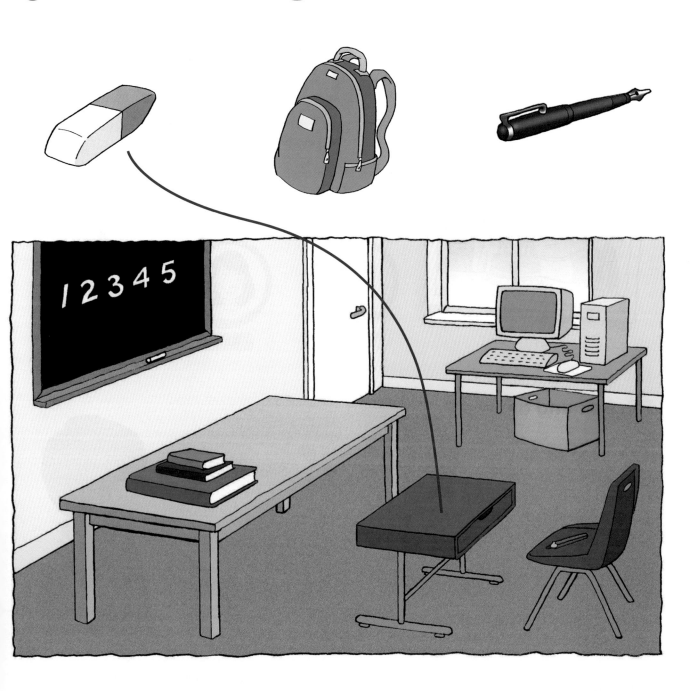

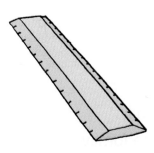

Listening PART 2

Step 1 – Prepare

1 Listen and write 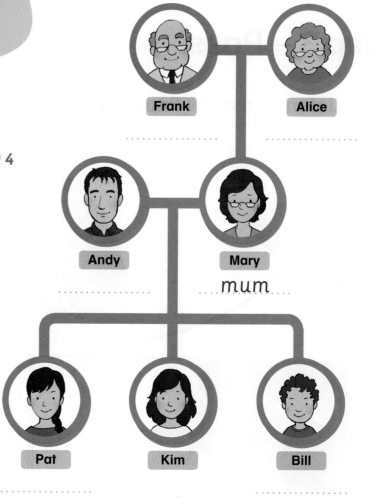 🎧 4
the family words.

mum

2 Ask and answer.

Who's Mary?

She's Kim's mum.

Who's Frank?

He's Kim's grandpa.

3 Write *T* (true) or *F* (false).

1	Kim has got two brothers.	F
2	Frank is Pat's cousin.	
3	Pat has got a brother and a sister.	
4	There are two girls in the family.	
5	There are three women in the family.	
6	Frank and Andy are men.	

Irregular plurals
one man – two **men**
one woman – two **women**

Remember!

4 **Draw lines.**

body

eye

nose

mouth

head

leg

arm

hair

foot

5 **Circle the correct words.**

1 Ben is **big** / **small**

2 He's got **long** / **short** hair.

3 He's **young** / **old**.

4 He's **smiling** / **waving**.

5 He's got **black** / **brown** hair.

6 He's got **big** / **small** feet.

Remember!

He's got ... = He has got ...
He's young. = He is young.

6 **Look and write** *is* / *isn't* **or**
's got / *hasn't got*.

1 This _____ is _____ Kim's grandma.
2 She _____ old.
3 She _____ grey hair.
4 She _____ long hair.
5 She _____ smiling.
6 She _____ sleeping.

Remember!

Step 2 – Practise

double = x2

double n = nn

1 Listen and write the names.  5

1 _ _ _ _   **2** Anna   3 _ _ _ _   4 _ _ _

2 Listen and write the numbers. 6

1 How old is Anna? ...... 7 ......
2 How many brothers has she got? ....
3 How old is Tom? ....
4 How many dogs have they got? ....
5 How many fish have they got? ....

Remember!

Write **7** not seven.

Step 3 – Pass!

1 Listen and write a name or a number.  7

1 What's the girl's name? .... Jill ....
2 How old is she? ....
3 How many sisters has she got? ....
4 What's her brother's name? ....
5 How old is he? ....
6 What's their dog's name? ....

Step 1 – Prepare

1 Listen and tick ✔ the sports Bill likes. 🎧 8
Cross ✘ the sports he doesn't like.

1 [ ]   2 [ ]   3 [ ]   4 [ ]   5 [✔]   6 [ ]

2 Ask and answer.

He likes football.
He likes **playing** football.

Remember!

Does Bill like playing tennis?

Yes, he does.

3 Look and write the words.

1 b a b s e t l k a l   .....basketball.....
2 n e t i n s   ....
3 t i n b d a n o m   ....
4 m i n s m w i g   ....
5 l o t o b a l f   ....
6 c e k y o h   ....

4 Circle the correct words.

1 He's riding **a bike** / **a horse**.

2 His bike is **blue and black** / **red and blue**.

3 He's got **black hair** / **brown hair**.

4 **He's wearing** / **He wears** a green T-shirt.

5 He's **singing** / **waving**.

6 He **likes** / **doesn't like** riding his bike.

5 Look and count. Write the numbers.

1 How many men are there? _____5_____

2 How many girls are there? ....

3 How many men are playing table tennis? ....

4 How many girls are playing hockey? ....

5 How many boys are playing football? ....

6 How many people are throwing a ball? ....

6 Look and write *is / isn't* or *are / aren't*.

> **Remember!**
>
> A man (He) is swimming.
>
> Two girls (They) are playing tennis.

1 A man ......*is*...... swimming.

2 Two men .... riding bikes.

3 Four boys .... playing football.

4 Two men are playing table tennis. They .... playing football.

5 A boy is playing basketball. He .... playing baseball.

6 Two girls .... playing tennis. They .... playing baseball.

Step 2 – Practise

1 Write *T* (true) or *F* (false).

1 She's sitting on a chair. ....T....
2 She's sitting on a chair playing the piano. ....
3 She's playing the guitar. ....
4 She's wearing blue trousers. ....
5 She isn't smiling. ....
6 She's sitting on a chair playing the guitar. ....

2 Listen and tick ✔ the correct picture. 🎧 9

Listen carefully! Then tick.

1 Which is Nick? A  ✔ B

2 What's Kim doing? A  B

3 What's Ben doing? A  B

4 What's Sue doing? A  B

Step 3 – Pass!

1 **Listen and tick ✔ the correct picture.**  10

1 What's Pat doing?

A    B    C ✔

2 Which is Sam's bike?

A    B    C

3 What can Nick do?

A    B    C

4 Which girl is Ann?

A 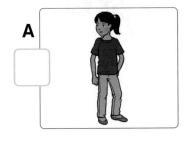   B    C

5 Where are Kim's shoes?

A 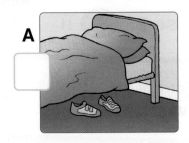   B    C

Step 1 – Prepare

1 Colour the crayons.

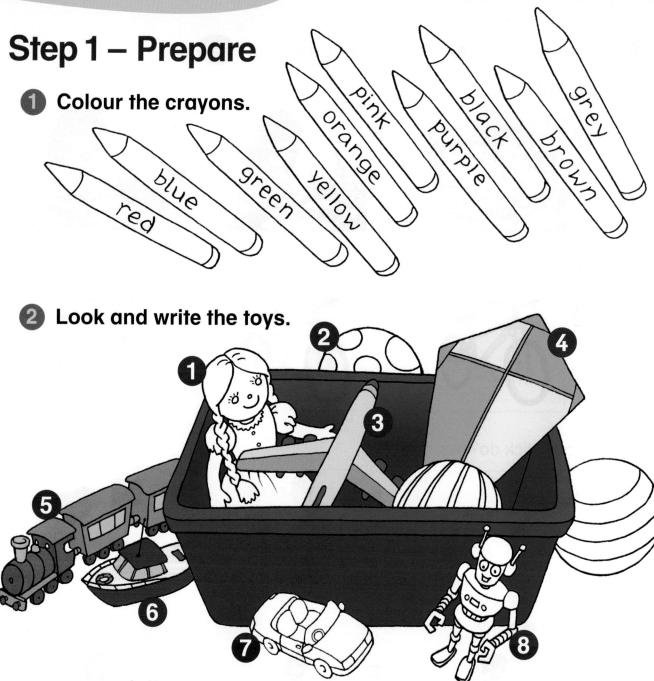

2 Look and write the toys.

1 .... doll	5 ....
2	6 ....
3	7 ....
4	8 ....

3 Listen and colour the picture in exercise 2. 11

Remember!

Listen for the prepositions:
in, on, under, behind …

4 **Write _T_ (true) or _F_ (false).**

1 The doll is next to the robot.   T
2 The car is between the ball and the train.   ....
3 The train is behind the robot.   ....
4 The kite is on the box.   ....
5 The box is next to the doll.   ....
6 The car is under the kite.   ....

Remember!

In front of ...

Next to ...

5 **Look and write.**

in
on
under
next to
between
~~in front of~~

1 The bed is _in front of_ the cupboard.
2 The robot is .... the box.
3 The ball is .... the bed.
4 The car is .... the cupboard.
5 The box is .... the bed and the bookcase.
6 The small picture is .... the bookcase .... the lamp.

Step 2 – Practise

1 Listen and colour. 12

Listen carefully. Don't colour everything!

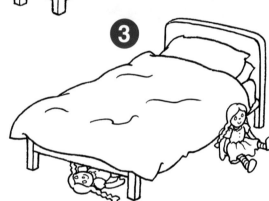

2 Work with a partner. Colour the toys. Then ask and answer.

Student A

Student B

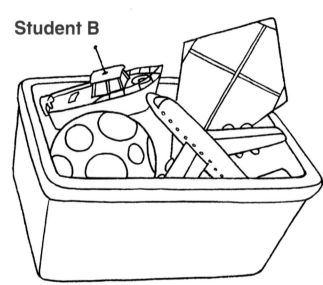

What colour is the lorry?

It's red.

Step 3 – Pass!

1 Listen and colour. 13

Step 1 – Prepare

1 Find nine transport words.

inbike t a k b o a t e g b u s e w c a r p l a n d e f t e k i b r o t o m a e y r r o l i m a r e t p o c i l e h t o l d n a l p t e k i b r o t o m a e g n i a r t s e t

2 Read and colour.

The motorbike is yellow. The lorry is blue.
The plane is grey and white. The train is purple.
The helicopter is red. The boat isn't red. It's green.

3 Look and write *This is a ...* or *These are ...*

1 .... This is a plane. ....

2 ....

3 ....

4 ....

5 ....

6 ....

Plural form	
one car	two cars
one lorry	two lorries

Remember!

4 Look and write.

bike   bus   car   motorbike   ~~plane~~

1   *plane*

2 ....

3 ....

4 ....

5 ....

5 Look at the picture in exercise 4. Write *T* (true) or *F* (false).

1 There are three cars.   .....T.....

2 The green car is in front of the bus.   ....

3 The motorbike is behind the red car.   ....

4 The plane is blue.   ....

5 There are two bikes.   ....

6 The black bike is between the green car and the blue car. ....

6 Look and write. Then ask and answer.

ride   riding   ~~drive~~   driving   fly   flying

1 Can your mum   *drive*   a car?

2 Do you like .... your bike?

3 Would you like to .... in a helicopter?

4 Can you .... a horse?

5 Does your Dad like .... his car to work?

6 Do you like .... in a plane?

Can your mum drive a car?

Yes, she can.

21

Step 2 – Practise

1 Tick ✔ the correct picture.

1 This is a motorbike.   **A** ✔    **B** ☐

2 This is a plane.   **A** ☐    **B** ☐

3 This is a boat.   **A** ☐    **B** ☐

4 This is a lorry.   **A** ☐    **B** ☐

2 Tick ✔ the correct word.

Remember!

This is (singular)
These are (plural)

1 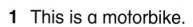   This is a   plane. ✔ / planes. ☐ / train. ☐

2   These are   a car. ☐ / cars. ☐ / buses. ☐

3  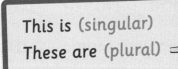   These are   motorbikes. ☐ / bikes. ☐ / bike. ☐

4    This is a   truck. ☐ / lorry. ☐ / train. ☐

Step 3 – Pass!

1 Look and read. Put a tick ✔ or a cross ✘ in the box.

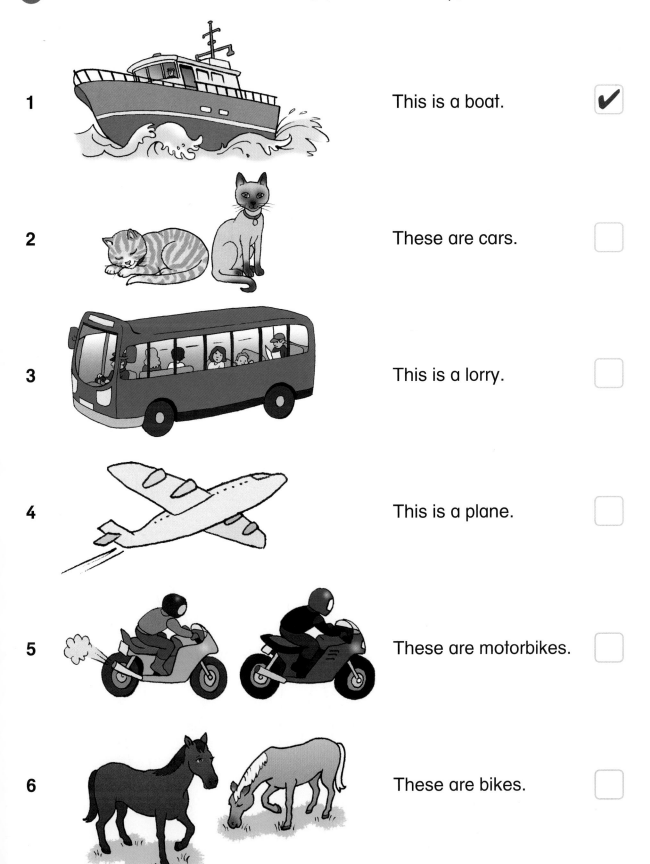

1	This is a boat.	✔
2	These are cars.	☐
3	This is a lorry.	☐
4	This is a plane.	☐
5	These are motorbikes.	☐
6	These are bikes.	☐

Step 1 – Prepare

1 **Find and write ten clothes words.**

v	t	k	l	s	d	e	w	a	p
b	z	r	o	g	r	i	w	m	l
f	q	u	o	j	e	d	n	r	e
c	h	m	t	u	s	h	i	r	t
j	e	a	n	s	s	k	u	v	s
a	s	b	t	h	y	e	c	w	k
c	i	o	s	x	r	q	r	j	i
k	h	d	c	s	h	o	e	s	r
e	n	u	t	k	f	s	v	i	t
t	x	c	a	t	s	h	i	r	t

1 .... dress ....
2 ....
3 ....
4 ....
5 ....
6 ....
7 ....
8 ....
9 ....
10 ....

> trousers and jeans are plural.

> Rememb

> Rememb

2 **Read, draw and colour the clothes on the boy.**

He's wearing a red T-shirt and blue trousers.
He isn't wearing a hat.
He's wearing black shoes.

3 **Draw clothes on the girl and write.**

1 She's wearing ....

2 She isn't wearing ....

4 **Look and write.**

1 The teacher is .... *wearing* .... a green skirt.

2 Three children .... writing in their books.

3 The boy behind the table is wearing blue ....

4 A boy in a green shirt is sitting .... a girl in a yellow T-shirt.

5 .... children are sitting down.

6 The teacher is wearing ....

5 **Look at the picture in exercise 4. Circle *yes* or *no*.**

1 The teacher has got a handbag. **yes /no**

2 She's wearing a pink shirt. **yes / no**

3 The children are wearing trousers. **yes / no**

4 The girl in the yellow T-shirt is wearing a watch. **yes / no**

5 The teacher is sitting down. **yes / no**

6 The teacher is holding a pen. **yes / no**

Who's wearing
a red shirt?

The boy behind
the table.

6 **Look at the picture in exercise 4. Ask and answer.**

1 Who's wearing a red shirt?

2 How many children are standing up?

3 How many people are holding a pen or a pencil?

4 Who's wearing green trousers?

5 How many children are wearing white shoes?

6 Who's holding a yellow pencil?

Step 2 – Practise

1 **Look and draw a line to match the sentence halves.**

1 The small boy		are smiling.
2 Two people		are sitting on the sofa.
3 Grandma		is wearing a yellow dress.
4 Mum		are eating ice cream.
5 Six people		is wearing a purple skirt.
6 Three people		is wearing a red T-shirt.

2 **Look and read. Write *yes* or *no*.**

1 Two girls are playing tennis. ......no......

2 They are wearing skirts. ....

3 They are wearing black shoes. ....

4 The boy and his grandpa are playing football. ....

5 Grandpa is wearing green shorts. ....

6 The boy is wearing an orange T-shirt. ....

Step 3 – Pass!

1 **Look and read. Write *yes* or *no*.**

1 Two girls are making a birthday cake. ......*yes*......

2 One girl is wearing a red T-shirt. ....

3 Dad is playing the piano. ....

4 Mum is wearing glasses. ....

5 The boy is watching television. ....

6 He's wearing a T-shirt. ....

Step 1 – Prepare

1 Do the crossword and find Ben's favourite food.

					b	r	e	a	d
1									
2	t								
3	b								
4	p								
5			o						
6	m								
7	f								

My favourite food is
_____.

2 Ask and answer.

Do you like bread?

Yes, I do.

3 Circle and write six fruits. Then find three more words and find Lucy's favourite lunch.

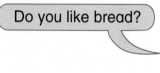  

peareggslemonsausageswatermelonlimeandmangochipsgrapes

1 p e a r
2 _ _ _ _ _ _
3 _ _ _ _ _ _ _ _ _ _
4 _ _ _ _ _
5 _ _ _ _ _
6 _ _ _ _ _ _

I like _ _ _ _ _ ,
_ _ _ _ _ _ _ _ _ _
and _ _ _ _ _ _ .

4 Look at the letters. Write the words.

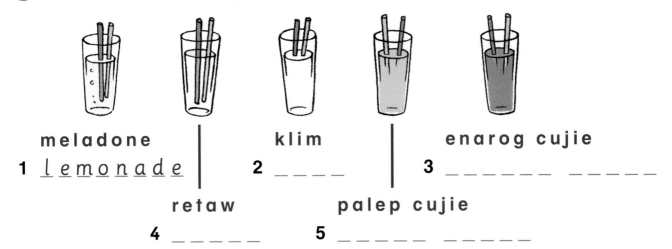

meladone
1 l e m o n a d e

2 k l i m
_ _ _ _

3 e n a r o g   c u j i e
_ _ _ _ _ _   _ _ _ _ _

4 r e t a w
_ _ _ _ _

5 p a l e p   c u j i e
_ _ _ _ _   _ _ _ _ _

5 Ask and answer.

What's your favourite drink?

I love apple juice.

6 Write three words in each column. Then ask and answer.

breakfast	lunch	dinner

What do you have for breakfast?

I have bread, fruit and orange juice.

Step 2 – Practise

1 **Write the missing letters. Draw lines.**

1 a p p <u>l e</u>
2 b _ r _ _ r
3 _ _ k _
4 p _ _ _
5 p _ _ e _ _ _ l _
6 _ c e _ r _ _ m

2 **Look at the pictures and letters. Write the words.**

1  d e r a b   <u>b r e a d</u>

2  t a r o c r   _ _ _ _ _ _

3 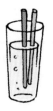 d a n o m e l e   _ _ _ _ _ _ _ _

4  c e n h k i c   _ _ _ _ _ _ _

5  n o c t u c o   _ _ _ _ _ _ _

Remember

Write one letter
on each dash:
<u>b r e a d</u>

6  s e g a s u a   _ _ _ _ _ _ _

Step 3 – Pass!

1 **Look at the pictures. Look at the letters. Write the words.**

1  keca   <u>c a k e</u>

2 rubreg   _ _ _ _ _ _

3 sepa   _ _ _ _

4  likm   _ _ _ _

5 cie rmeac   _ _ _ _ _ _ _ _

6  phics   _ _ _ _ _

Step 1 – Prepare

1 **Write the parts of the body. Then draw lines.**

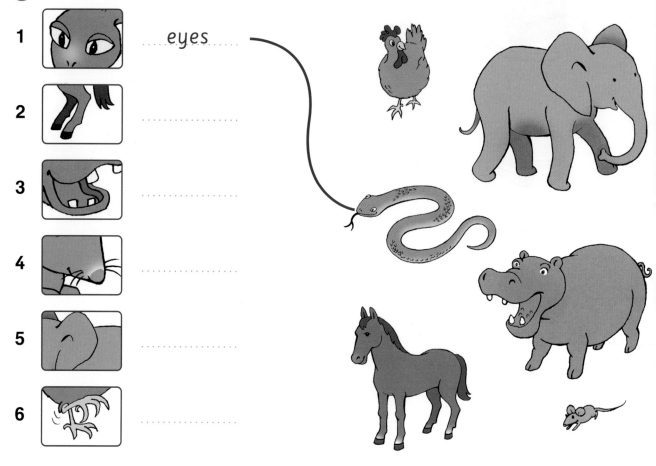

1 .....eyes......

2 ....

3 ....

4 ....

5 ....

6 ....

2 **Ask and answer.**

What's number 1?

It's a snake.

3 **Circle the correct words.**

1 Birds can **fly** / **talk**.
2 Frogs can **jump** / **fly**.
3 Fish can **walk** / **swim**.
4 Hippos can **swim** / **fly**.
5 Horses can **sing** / **run**.
6 Crocodiles can **swim** / **jump**.

4 **Look and write the words.**

ducks	**1** ....Cats........	catch mice.
tigers	**2**	can fly.
elephants	**3**	have got two arms and two legs.
monkeys	**4**	haven't got any legs.
snakes	**5**	eat meat.
~~cats~~	**6**	are very big.

5 **Write _T_ (true) or _F_ (false).**

1 Horses have got four legs. ....T....

2 Chickens can swim. ....

3 Elephants don't eat meat. ....

4 Cats live in houses. ....

5 Dogs drink orange juice. ....

6 Cats don't eat fish. ....

6 **Write _horse_, _fish_ or _bird_. Then play a game.**

1 You can ride me. ....horse..........

2 I can swim. ....

3 I can fly. ....

4 I've got two legs. ....

5 I eat carrots. ....

6 I live in water. ....

Can you fly?

No, I can't.

Can you swim?

Yes, I can.

Are you a fish?

Yes, I am!

Step 2 – Practise

1 **Circle the correct words.**

1 I've got four **leg** / **legs** / **head**.
2 I drink **carrots** / **water** / **hair**.
3 I don't live in a **houses** / **horse** / **house**.
4 You can **swim** / **ride** / **today** me.
5 I've got big **eye** / **eyes** / **ear**.
6 I am a **horse** / **horses** / **animal**.

2 **Look and read. Write the words.**

| apples | bird | water | fish | ~~tree~~ | horse | legs | sea |

1 I live in a .... tree ....

I've got two ....

I can fly. I'm a ....

> Copy the words carefully!

2 I live in the ....

I can swim. I'm a ....

3 I'm big. I've got four legs. I like eating ....

I drink ....

I'm a ....

Step 3 – Pass!

1 **Read and choose a word from the box.**
Write the correct word next to numbers 1–5.

I've got two legs and two .... *arms* .... I've got two eyes,

a nose, a mouth and two big **1** .... I live in

2 .... I like eating **3** ....

I can run and I can **4** .... I can hold

a **5** .... but I can't write.

What am I? I am a monkey.

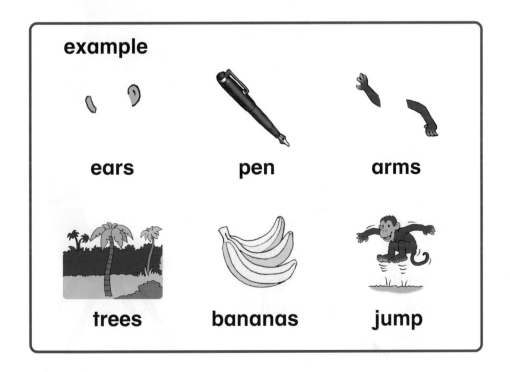

Step 1 – Prepare

1 **Look and read. Write the words.**

| house | park | zoo | ~~shop~~ | school | beach |

1 .... shop ....

2 ....

3 ....

4 ....

5 ....

6 ....

In my street there is a park, a school, a shop and a zoo. My house is next to the school. The school is between my house and the park. My house is between the shop and the school. The park is next to the zoo. The zoo is between the park and the beach. I love my street!

2 **Ask and answer.**

Where's the school?

It's between the house and the park.

3 **Circle the odd word.**

1	park	zoo	(chair)
2	next to	shop	between
3	classroom	playing	playground
4	clock	afternoon	morning
5	house	book	apartment
6	night	school	shop

4 Circle the correct words.

1	Where are they?	(at the beach) / having a picnic
2	How many children are in the sea?	swimming / two
3	What's the dog doing?	run / watching the children
4	Where's the snake?	in the tree / yes, there is
5	What colour is the bag?	red / a red bag
6	What are mum and dad doing?	eat / eating

Answer -ing questions with -ing answers.

Remember!

5 Look and write.

three	house	next to	sea	~~two~~	bag

1	How many girls are there?	.... two ....
2	Where is the boy?	in the ....
3	How many people are eating?	....
4	Where's the dog?	.... the sea
5	Where's the mat?	next to the ....
6	What's at the end of the beach?	a ....

6 Ask and answer.

How many girls are there?

There's one.

37

Step 2 – Practise

1 **Look at the pictures and write *a* or *b*.**

1 The children are going to the zoo. ....*a*........

2 There's a monkey. ....

3 There are six children. ....

4 Two girls are walking. ....

5 The boy in the orange T-shirt is behind the girl in the blue T-shirt. ....

6 There are two ice creams. ....

2 **Look at the pictures in exercise 1. Read and write one-word answers.**

Write on~ word onl~

Picture a

1 How many girls are there? ....2............

2 Where are they going? to the ....

3 Which animal can you see? an ....

Picture b

4 Who is eating a pink ice cream? the ....

5 What is the girl holding? an ....

6 Is the boy in the yellow T-shirt happy? ....

Step 3 – Pass!

1 Look at the pictures and read the questions.
   Write one-word answers.

1 How many children are there? .... 3 ....

2 Where are they?   at the ....

3 Who is kicking the ball?   the ....

4 What colour is the sea?   ....

5 What has the dog got?   a ....

6 What is the dog doing?   it's ....

Speaking PARTS **1-5**

Step 1 – Prepare

1 **Write the words in the best place.**

in the park	**in the street**	**at the beach**
trees	bus	shells

2 **Ask and answer.**

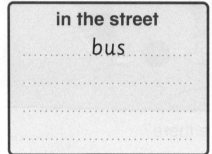

Where's + singular noun

Where are + plural noun

Remember!

 Where's the rabbit?

It's in the park.

3 **Write the words in order. Then write *p* (park), *s* (street) or *b* (beach**

1 flying / a / boy / kite / A / is

  A boy is flying a kite.   p

2 are / There / lots / cars / of

3 sea / woman / A / swimming / in / is / the

4 three / There / shells / are

5 are / Two / eating / ducks / bread

6 of / man / a / shop / in / A / standing / front / is

40

4 Read and draw.

1 Draw a cat in front of the cupboard.
2 Draw a camera between the cake and the apples.
3 Draw a lemon on the table next to the apples.
4 Draw a coconut in the cupboard under the lemonade.
5 Draw a picture on the wall behind the boy.
6 Draw a watch on the girl's arm.

5 Circle the correct answer.

1 What's your name?   **My name Ann. /(Anne.)**
2 How old are you?   **I'm eight. / I seven.**
3 What's your friends name? **Jenny. / She Jenny.**
4 Is your house big or small? **Is big. / It's big.**
5 Can you play table tennis? **Yes, I can. / No, can't.**
6 Have you got a dog?   **No. / Yes, it is.**

Short answers
are OK!

6 Ask and answer the questions in exercise 5.

What's your name?

May.

41

Step 2 – Practise

1 **Look at the picture. Find and circle.**

a dog
a monkey
a book
a hat
a ball
an apple
a radio
a cat

2 **Ask, answer and point.**

Where's the dog?

It's here. It's behind the horse.

3 **Count and write. Then ask and answer.**

1 ducks ....3............
2 flowers ....
3 children ....
4 animals ....
5 girls ....
6 boys ....

How many ducks are there?

Three.

4 Ask and answer.

1 What's the boy doing?
2 What's the girl in the hat doing?
3 What colour is the woman's bag?
4 What's the girl under the tree doing?
5 What colour is the kite?
6 What's the man doing?

What's the boy doing?

He's flying a kite.

5 Write the words in order. Then match answers to the questions.

1 your / name / What's / ?
   What's your name? ....c....
2 old / How / you / are / ?
   ....
3 many / brothers / have / sisters / and / How / you / got / ?
   ....
4 favourite / your / What's / colour / ?
   ....
5 like / Do / swimming / you / ?
   ....
6 tennis / you / Can / play / ?
   ....

a Yes, I do.
b I've got one brother and two sisters.
c My name's Emma.
d Blue.
e No, I can't.
f I'm eight.

Remember!

Say 'Hello', 'Goodbye' and 'Thank you' to the examiner.

6 Ask and answer the questions in exercise 5.

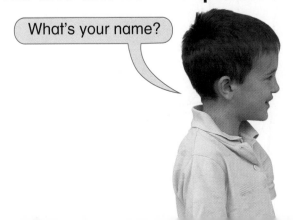

What's your name?

My name's Emma.

Step 3 – Pass!

Listening

Part 1 (5 questions)

Listen and draw lines. There is one example. 14

Listening

Part 2 (5 questions)

Read the questions. Listen and write a name or a number. There are two examples. 15

Examples

What's Kim's friend's name? .... Alex ....

How old is Alex? .... 7 ....

Listening

Part 2 (5 questions)

Questions

1 How many sisters has Alex got? ....

2 Which class are the children in at school? ....

3 Who's reading? ....

4 Who has got a green pencil? ....

5 How many children can draw? ....

Listening

Part 3 (5 questions)

Listen and tick ✔ the box. There is one example. 16

Which is Bill?

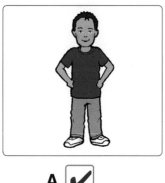

A ✔

B ☐

C ☐

1 What's Ann's favourite fruit?

A ☐

B ☐

C ☐

2 What is Pat doing?

A ☐

B ☐

C ☐

3 Where's Tony's kite?

A ☐

B ☐

C ☐

4 What are the cats doing?

A ☐

B ☐

C ☐

5 Which bike is Ann's?

A ☐

B ☐

C ☐

Listening

Part 4 (5 questions)

Listen and colour. There is one example. 17

Reading & Writing

Part 1 (5 questions)

Look and read. Put a tick ✔ or a cross ✘ in the box.
There are two examples.

Examples

This is a doll.   ☑

This is a cow.   ☒

Questions

1   This is a guitar.   ☐

2   This is a sofa. ☐

3   This is a goat. ☐

4   This is an orange. ☐

5   This is a plane. ☐

Reading & Writing

Part 2 (5 questions)

Look and read. Write *yes* or *no*.

Examples

The pink monster is big.	....yes....
There are two dogs in the picture.	......no.....

1 There are five monsters in the picture.   ....

2 The green monster has got a kite.   ....

3 The yellow monster is sleeping.   ....

4 The red monster is under a tree.   ....

5 The dog has got a blue ball.   ....

Reading & Writing

Part 3 (5 questions)

Look at the pictures. Look at the letters. Write the words.

Example

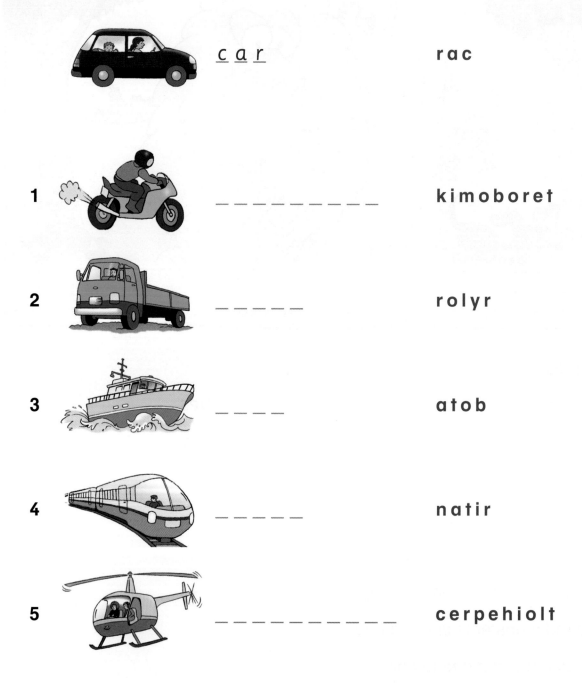

c a r   r a c

1 _ _ _ _ _ _ _ _ _   k i m o b o r e t

2 _ _ _ _ _   r o l y r

3 _ _ _ _   a t o b

4 _ _ _ _ _   n a t i r

5 _ _ _ _ _ _ _ _ _ _   c e r p e h i o l t

Reading & Writing

Part 4 (5 questions)

Read this. Choose a word from the box. Write the correct word next to the numbers 1–5. There is one example.

I'm a small animal. I've got four ....*legs*........ , two ears, two

eyes and a tail. I live in a (1) .... with a family.

At (2) .... I sleep in my (3) ....

but in the day I sleep on the (4) .... I like playing

in the (5) ....

example

| legs | carrots | bed | night |
| garden | sofa | house | guitar |

Reading & Writing

Part 5 (5 questions)

Look at the pictures and read the questions.
Write one-word answers.

Examples

Where are they?   in the .... *kitchen* ....

What are they doing?   making a .... *cake* ....

1 What has the boy got?   a ....

PRACTICE TEST

2 Who is opening the door? ....

3 Who is behind Mum? the ....

4 Where's the dog? .... the table

5 What is the dog eating? the ....

Speaking
Summary of Procedures

The usher introduces the child to the examiner.

1 The examiner familiarises the child with the picture first and then asks the child to point out certain items on the scene picture, e.g. 'Where's the television?'

2 The examiner asks the child to put the object cards in various locations on the scene picture, e.g. 'Put the lamp on the bookcase.'

3 The examiner asks questions about two of the people of things in the scene picture, e.g. 'What's this?' (Answer: a clock) 'What colour is it?' (Answer: blue)

4 The examiner asks questions about the object card, e.g. 'What's this?' (Answer: a cat) and 'Have you got a cat?'

5 The examiner asks questions about the child, e.g. 'How old are you?'

Practise and Pass
Young Learners English Test

STARTERS

....

took the Practise and Pass Starters Test

on

....

at

....

Listening ☆☆☆☆☆

Reading & Writing ☆☆☆☆☆

Speaking ☆☆☆☆☆

Signed

....